# *A Thousand Splendid Suns*

## by Khaled Hosseini

## A Study Guide by Ray Moore

**Acknowledgements:**
Where I have selectively quoted from the writings of others in the course of my own argument, I have done so in the sincere belief that this constitutes Fair Use. I will immediately remove any quotation if requested to do so.

*A Thousand Splendid Suns* by Khaled Hosseini

# Contents

*A Thousand Splendid Suns* by Khaled Hosseini

# Teacher's Introduction

# Plot Summary:

This novel tells the story of two women born in Afghanistan in the second half of the twentieth century. Mariam, born in Herat in the 1960s, is the illegitimate daughter of a wealthy businessman who refuses to recognize her as part of his family who is brought up by her embittered mother; Laila, born in Kabul in the 1970s, is the daughter of intellectual parents who teach her the value of education and inspire her to want to make a contribution to improving society. Circumstances bring these two different women together as the wives of Rasheed, a shoemaker in Kabul. Initially hostile to each other, Mariam and Laila gradually forge a deep friendship in the face both of the increasing violence of their husband and the deteriorating political and military situation in their country. Together they face adversities which at times reduce them to helplessness in the face of forces over which they have no control.

# Why Read this Book?

This novel was a number one *New York Times* bestseller for fifteen-weeks.

Above all, this is a well written novel. It avoids clichés and easy solutions. Anyone who has read *The Kite Runner* will not be disappointed by what I think is an even better book. Hosseini told Time magazine, "I never thought it [fiction] was about writing things that everybody agrees about, that make everybody feel warm and fuzzy inside." This novel certainly deals with complex issues which have no simple answers.

The novel looks at Islam in a critical way, yet from the perspective of one who respects its central teachings. Readers will definitely increase their understandings of the different sects within Islam and particularly of the fundamentalist traditionalism which leads to violent jihad and the imposition of brutal Shari'a Law. He/she will also learn of more progressive forms of Islam which value the education of women and see women as essential members of the workforce in creating a prosperous community.

Hosseini says, "I had been entertaining the idea of writing a story of Afghan women for some time after I'd finished writing The Kite Runner. That first novel was a male-dominated story. All the major characters, except perhaps for Amir's wife Soraya, were men. There was a whole facet of Afghan society which I hadn't touched on in The Kite Runner, an entire landscape that I felt was fertile with story ideas" (Book Browse Interview).

**Important: Issues with this Book.**

The novel was clearly written for an adult audience, but having said that it contains little bad language and no graphic descriptions of sex, though sexual acts do occur. There are descriptions of horrific violence both in the context of the fighting in and around Kabul and of the abusive marriage in which Mariam and Laila are trapped.

**A Note on the graphic organizers:**

Two graphic organizers are provided to enable the students to make notes. Some simple guidance will be needed depending on how the teacher wants them to be used.

## Map of Afghanistan.

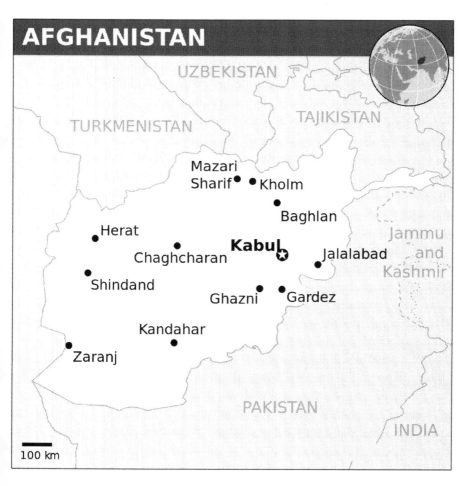

*Spoiler alert!*
*If you are reading the novel for the first time, you may wish to go straight*
*to the Study Questions and come back to this section later.*

# Dramatis Personæ

*Mariam's 'family' and acquaintances:*

**Jalil** - Mariam is Jalil's illegitimate daughter. He is a wealthy businessman who owns a movie theater in the town of Herat. He has three legitimate wives with whom he has fathered ten legitimate children; Mariam is the child of an affair he had with a maid in his house. Mariam idolizes Jalil, looking forward to his weekly visits, but her mother is bitter about the way in which he has, in order to protect his reputation, made both her and her daughter outcasts not only from his family but also from society. Mariam dreams of living in Jalil's house, and getting to know her brothers and sisters, but Nana knows that Jalil is never going to let this happen. When Nana commits suicide, Mariam is taken to Jalil's house, but his other wives will not allow her to become a member of their family and he does not have the courage to stand up to them. Arrangements are made for her to marry Rasheed a much older man who lives in Kabul. Jalil is essentially a weak man who lacks the courage of his convictions and feelings; years later he regrets his harsh treatment of Mariam, and attempts to reconcile with her. He dies in 1987, leaving Mariam a legacy with Mullah Faizullah.

**Nana** - Nana is Mariam's mother with whom she lives in a "kolba" (shack) in a clearing outside of Herat. She suffers from "jinn," occasional (perhaps epileptic) seizures the onset of which caused her proposed wedding to be called off by the groom's family when she was fifteen. Nana worked as Jalil's housemaid until she became pregnant with his baby after which he cast her out of his household and built her the shack. Nana's life revolves around her role as Mariam's mother: it is the only role left to her since she will never be a wife. Thus, Nana discourages Mariam's attempts to get close to her father, and, when her daughter defies her in this, she kills herself convinced that she has lost Mariam.

**Mariam** - Mariam (an ethnic Tajik) is born in 1959 and grows up in the small shack with only her mother and a few regular visitors for company. Although her mother loves her very much, Nana has been made bitter by the way in which life (in particular Jalil) has treated her. She raises Mariam very strictly which the ambitious Mariam resents. Unaware of the way he has mistreated her mother, Mariam idolizes her natural father

Jalil, who visits and spends time with her every Thursday. She dreams of being a part of his family and of going to see a movie in his cinema, but her attempts to make these dreams a reality result in her mother's suicide, rejection by Jalil's family, and an arranged marriage to a much older man, Rasheed, who lives in Kabul. Mariam suffers deeply from the stigma of being a bastard and from the guilt she feels over her mother's death; together these rob her of her sense of self-worth. Hosseini has written, 'The key word with Mariam is that she is isolated in every sense of the word. She is a woman who is detached from the day-to-day norms of human existence. Really, she just wants connection with another human being" (Denver Post Interview).

**Bibi Jo** - Nana's friend, Bibi Jo, regularly visits their small shack and Mariam likes to listen to her complaints and gossip.

**Mullah Faizullah** - Mariam's unofficial tutor is a Sufi (i.e., a Muslim mystic). He teaches her to read and the values embodied in the Koran. Mullah Faizullah is one of those Muslims who firmly believes in the education women. After Nana's suicide, Mariam begs Jalil to be allowed to live with Mullah Faizullah, but he refuses saying that the man is too old. Mariam will never see him again, but Jalil will leave with him a legacy which Laila will receive when she returns to Afghanistan and visits him. He dies in 1989.

*Jalil's legitimate family:*

**Khadija**, **Afsoon** and **Nargis** - Jalil's legitimate wives. When an orphaned Mariam is brought to Jalil's home, his wives make it clear that she cannot stay because she is illegitimate. The wives are behind the arranged marriage which will take Mariam hundreds of miles from Herat. Afsoon locks the door to Mariam's room so that she cannot run away.

**Nilofaur** - Afsoon's daughter is eight years old when Mariam is brought to Jalil's house. She is the only person in the house who is kind and welcoming to Mariam. Nilofaur tells Mariam that her mother said that Mariam was not really her sister but assures Mariam that she does not mind if Mariam *is* her sister. Nilofaur's attempts at friendship find little response in the traumatized Mariam.

**Muhsin**, **Farhad** and **Ramin** - Each month, two of Jalil's sons bring rations to Nana and Mariam so that Nana will not have to go into town to shop. Nana throws rocks at the boys when they come to the *kolba*, but Mariam feels rather sorry for them having to push the provisions in a wheelbarrow.

## *Characters in Kabul:*

**Rasheed** - The man chosen to be Mariam's husband (an ethnic Pashtun) is already in his mid-forties. He owns a shoe repair shop in Kabul, so in marrying him Mariam will leave Herat for good, which is just what Jalil's wives want. Rasheed is a complex character. He has already lost his first wife and his son drowned; it is rumored while he was himself too drunk to save the boy. At times, Rasheed can show tenderness and consideration but he is also very stern and has a quick temper. When he first marries Mariam, he hopes that she will give him a son but after a series of miscarriages he gives up hope and any affection he had for Mariam dies. From the start, he requires Mariam to wear the burqa when appearing in public and not to leave the house unless she does so with him. Ironically he is not himself a devout Muslim. Rasheed becomes increasingly abusive to his wives (Mariam and Laila) beating them severely. When Laila's parents are killed he immediately sees the chance of making her dependent upon him and sets about trapping her into marriage. He succeeds, and Laila becomes his third wife. Hosseini has said, "Rasheed's the embodiment of the patriarchal, tribal character. In writing him, I didn't want to write him as an irredeemable villain. He is a reprehensible person but there are moments of humanity, such as his love for his son" (Denver Post Interview).

**Khadim** - Khadim is a bully in Laila's neighborhood. One day, he squirts her with urine. Laila's childhood friend Tariq beats Khadim up for doing it, and after that Khadim leaves Laila alone.

## *Laila's family:*

**Hakim** - Laila's father is a rather impractical, idealistic man, an intellectual who loves books and study. He supports women's education and instills in Laila the desire to make a contribution to Afghan society. Hakim loves his country and its history valuing all of the cultures which have contributed to it. Having held on in Kabul as long as possible, he finally decides to leave when Laila is almost killed on the streets of Kabul. He and his wife die in the bomb blast as they are making preparations to leave.

**Fariba** - Hakim's wife lives on the same street in Kabul as does Rasheed and she tries, unsuccessfully, to befriend Mariam when she first arrives. Fariba has been worn down by the increasing violence in Afghanistan and particularly by the decision of her two sons to join the jihad. When she learns of their deaths, she is devastated.

**Ahmad** and **Noor** - Laila's elder brothers leave to fight in the jihad against the Soviets and are killed. Fariba is determined to stay in Kabul to see the freedom for which her sons died, but she agrees to move when life there becomes too dangerous.

**Laila** - The daughter of Hakim and Fariba (an ethnic Tajik) is raised in a liberal family at a time when Kabul is free of the restrictions on women imposed by traditional Islamic teaching. Laila's constant childhood companion is Tariq with whom, as a teenager, she falls in love. However, following the death of her parents, and after having been told that Tariq had been killed, she has no one else to protect her. Knowing herself to be pregnant with Tariq's child, she agrees to become Rasheed's third wife (his second living wife). After initial friction, Mariam becomes a surrogate mother to Laila - the loving, self-sacrificing mother than Laila never actually had.

**Hasina** and **Giti** - Laila's two school friends and playmates talk a lot about growing up and the lives they will lead. Hasina marries and emigrates from Afghanistan. Giti is killed by a shell on the streets of Kabul.

**Tariq** - Born in 1976, Laila's childhood friend and neighbor, Tariq (an ethnic Pashtun), lost a leg in a landmine explosion, but he never lets his disability hinder or define him. As they develop into adolescence Tariq and Laila fall in love, but Tariq's family decides that Kabul is too dangerous. Tariq begs Laila to escape with him but she feels obliged to stay with her family. The two conceive a child, but by the time Laila realizes she is pregnant, Tariq has gone and Laila's father and mother have been killed. Rasheed, who treats Laila well, pays a man to tell her that Tariq has died, so she feels that she has no alternative but to accept Rasheed's proposal of marriage. Tariq spends several years in prison in Pakistan, but he eventually returns to Kabul to find Laila.

**Aziza** - Laila's daughter is born in 1993 about eight months after her marriage to Rasheed who is disappointed that the child is not a boy and has growing suspicions that he may not be the father. Aziza is a delightful child and is a catalyst in the developing friendship between Mariam, whom she adores, and Laila. After Rasheed's shop is destroyed by fire and the family is running out of money, Rasheed decides to put Aziza into an orphanage and Laila is helpless to prevent it. In the orphanage, Aziza begins to develop a slight stammer, a sign of the trauma of separation from her family, but she also gets some education.

**Zalmai** - Laila's and Rasheed's son, born in 1997, is the heir for whom Rasheed hoped and he is good to the boy who, in turn, idolizes his father. Obedient to Laila and Mariam when his father is not present, he becomes defiant in his father's presence. It is Zalmai who tells Rasheed about Laila talking with Tariq, to whom he takes an instant dislike, which causes Rasheed to beat Laila to near death. When Tariq, Laila and Aziza make their escape from Kabul, Zalmai is anxious: he keeps asking where his father is and refuses to accept Tariq. Ultimately, however, Zalmai forgets Rasheed and begins to accept Tariq as a father.

**Zaman** - The director of the orphanage where Aziza stays is an enlightened man genuinely trying to do the best he can to protect and educate the children in his care irrespective of their gender. When Laila and Tariq return to Kabul, they work closely with Zaman to improve facilities at the orphanage.

## *Characters important at the end of the novel:*

**Salim** - Tariq spends several years in a Pakistani prison for having (innocently) attempted to smuggle hashish. There he becomes very close to Salim. When Tariq ends his sentence, Salim recommends Tariq to his brother Sayeed, who owns a hotel. Sayeed hires Tariq to work at the hotel.

**Sayeed** - Salim's brother, who owns a hotel and employs Tariq, Sayeed is impressed by Tariq's work ethic and treats him generously even enabling him to get a new prosthetic leg. Laila and Tariq spend a happy year working in Sayeed's hotel and recovering from the traumas they have all suffered.

**Hamza** - Mullah Faizullah's son is able to tell Laila about his father's death when she visits Herat. He gives her a box that Jalil left for Mariam which contains (amongst other things) enough money for Laila and her family to establish themselves in Kabul.

# Themes

There are many ways in which the themes of this novel could be described. The novel is certainly about 'Man's Inhumanity to Man' and it certainly illustrates the maxim that 'Power Corrupts." However, these categories seem too general. Though there are universal themes in the narrative, it is a story set in a specific time and place. Hosseini has said, "*The Kite Runner* was a father-son story, and *A Thousand Splendid Suns* can be seen as a mother-daughter story" (BookBrowse Interview).

## Love of Afghanistan

Many characters feel a deep sense of pride in being Afghanis. They are drawn not merely to the physical country which is their home, but to its rich history and its cultural traditions. Faced with the collapse into violence and religious repression of the place they love (most often in this novel Kabul) they stay long after it is safe for them to do so and return as soon as they can. These characters are always progressives who see the return to strict Shari'a Law as the negation of everything in which they believe. Laila, who has been raised by her father to believe that a country needs educated women, feels an urge to return to Kabul and contribute to the restoration after the defeat of the Taliban. They dream of an Islamic nation which recognizes the rights of all citizens irrespective of gender or class, a peaceful country in which parents can bring up their children.

## The Importance of Reputation in Afghanistan Society

In Afghan culture, having a blameless reputation is much more important than acting blamelessly, at least for the men. Thus, young men are expected to have sexual encounters and are not condemned for them but when a young woman is found to have done the same thing she is ruined for life because no man will marry her. This is a culture of dual standards. Thus, when Jalil finds out that he has made his housekeeper pregnant he casts her out of his house. Despite his evident love for Mariam, Jalil cannot bring himself to make her a part of his family after her mother's death and marries her off to a much older man who lives hundreds of miles away.

## The Conflict Between Fundamentalist and Liberal Islam

Underpinning the entire novel is a battle over what it means to be a Muslim. The very forces which liberate Afghanistan from the foreign political and military oppression of the Soviet Union impose a religious and cultural repression which originates in a fundamentalist interpretation of Islam. Very clearly, the author sees this tendency as a violation not only of the rights and liberties of individuals but as a misreading of the Koran. His sympathies throughout are with those who have enlightened views, those who value education, and those who value the full heritage of Afghanistan. The characters who impose Shari'a Law are shown to be brutal, sadistic and often hypocritical. Hosseini has said, "The Taliban's acts of cultural vandalism—the most infamous being the destruction of the giant Bamiyan Buddhas—had a devastating effect on Afghan culture and the artistic scene" (Book Browse Interview)

## The Position of Women in Afghanistan Society / The Importance of Education

Hosseini has said, "In the spring of 2003, I went to Kabul, and I recall seeing these burqa-clad women sitting at street corners, with four, five, six children, begging for change. I remember watching them walking in pairs up the street, trailed by their children in ragged clothes, and wondering how life had brought them to that point...I spoke to many of those women in Kabul. Their life stories were truly heartbreaking" (Book Browse Interview).

In the 1980s and early 1990s, women in Afghanistan (and particularly those living in the capital, Kabul) had the right to education and to employment. That all changed in 1996 when the Taliban came to power and instituted laws which took away virtually all rights from women. Punishments for breaking these rules were swift and brutal. Even after the fall of the Taliban, the situation of women in Afghanistan did not greatly improve because repression had become deeply imbedded in Islamic culture and the government had neither the power not the will to protect women. [Note: The GradeSaver Study Guide has an excellent section "Women in Afghanistan" that I recommend.]

To simplify, two cultural traditions are in conflict in this novel. Islamic traditionalists believe (or pretend to believe) that women are incapable of education because their brains work differently from the brains of men. In contrast, there is a core of Islamists who support the education of women. Traditionalists insist that women stay in the house, that they only go out when accompanied by a male family member and that in public they wear the burqa. As a child, a woman is virtually the property of the father and as a wife of the husband; husbands are expected to be strict with their wives and beat them when necessary. Mullah Faizullah is a more liberal

Muslim who teaches Mariam the Koran and how to read and write. In contrast, Nana, who has all of her life been the victim of the traditionalists, sees no point in Mariam attending school; for Nana, all that a woman needs to know in life is how to "endure." Laila's father constantly stresses the importance of her education because he believes that to be a successful country Afghanistan will need to make use of all of its citizens. This is why Laila teaches at the orphanage school.

**Victimization of Women in Patriarchal Marriage / Spousal Abuse**
Almost all of the marriages recorded in the novel are arranged by the parents of the bride with or without her consent. Although the Muslim marriage service insists on the agreement to marry of the bride-to-be, the pressures that can be placed upon young girls by their family make acceptance of the man automatic. In selecting a marriage partner for a daughter, parents consider religious and ethnic compatibility, class, reputation and wealth above the girl's own feelings. Sometimes, of course, parents chose a man whom their daughter can love, or at least respect, but often they can do neither. Within marriage, men are given total power over their wives. At the age of fifteen, for example, Mariam was to marry a young man to whom she was attracted but when she suffered a fit it was the family of the groom that cancelled the wedding, so it seems that in the arranged marriage system males have little more freedom than do females. In contrast to the above is the love match between Laila and Tariq. With Tariq, Laila finds that sex, which Rasheed forced upon her, is actually making love, an activity in which each person is sensitive to the needs and feelings of the other. In her marriage, she is an equal partner, respected by a husband who wants her to have her own life.

**Children in Afghanistan Society**
Child birth and child rearing are very different in Afghanistan because women do not have access to adequate medical services. Thus, because Laila's baby cannot be delivered naturally she has to have an emergency caesarian operation without anesthetic and is very fortunate to survive. Even if a child is born safely infant mortality rates are staggeringly high. Rasheed tells Laila, "'They say that in Afghanistan one out of four children will die before the age of five'" (215). Largely because of the uncertainty of children growing to adulthood, a woman's value in Afghan society is largely measured by her ability to bear children, particularly sons. Thus, Rasheed loses all concern for Mariam when she has repeated miscarriages and is very disappointed when Laila's baby turns out to be a

girl. In the account of Zalmai's childhood we see how patriarchal attitudes are perpetuated: he loves and seeks to emulate his father by showing defiance to Laila and Mariam.

Nevertheless, despite the dangers of pregnancy, the pain of childbirth, and the difficulty of bringing up children, the love of mothers for their children is celebrated throughout the novel. Thus, by the end of her life, Mariam understands how much Nana loved her despite the fact that she was not always able to show that love; Mariam, herself unable to have children, learns what it feels to be a mother when she takes care of Aziza; and Laila realizes that she loves her son, Zalmai, whose father she hates, just as much as she loves the daughter whose father, Tariq, she loved.

## Love
Because they face oppression by Shari'a Law, by the civil government and by their husbands, women forge strong bonds of mutual support and friendship. When Laila becomes Rasheed's second wife, Mariam fears the loss of her status and reacts by taking out her bitterness on Laila. However, Mariam eventually realizes that she and Laila are equally victims of Rasheed's brutality, and they form a familial bond: Mariam becomes a mother-figure. Mariam shows the depth of her love for Laila and Aziza by sacrificing her own life to save them.

## Hope for a Better Future
The main characters in the novel, Mariam and Laila, have great hopes for their lives, but their dreams are repeatedly shattered. Mariam is finally defeated, though she remains defiant: aware that she can achieve nothing in her life, she sacrifices herself to give Laila hope. Laila returns to Kabul because she feels that she should make a contribution to rebuilding society.

"The personal stories of hope ... are mirrored in the political hope of the Afghan citizens. With every new ruler, people express their conviction that finally Afghanistan will be free. Yet, similar to the personal hope of individuals, Afghanistan's hope often turns to despair after the realities of each new regime leave the nation unfree" (GradeSaver).

*A Thousand Splendid Suns* by Khaled Hosseini

## Two Ways of Representing the Narrative in Graphic Form

Readers will find it helpful to use a timeline and a family tree each of which will help them to understand the relationships between the characters and the historical context in which the personal lives of the characters play out.

**Timeline:** The history of Afghanistan begins with the bloodless coup against King Zahir Shah who had ruled for forty years (Chapter 4).

**Family Tree:** The lives of Mariam (which begins with the union of Jalil and his housekeeper) and of Laila (which begins with the marriage of Hakim and Fariba) are united by their marriage to Rasheed.

NOTE

The timeline and family tree diagram are provided for the general reader later in the guide.

## Note for teachers

Since it would be too much to ask each student to produce both a timeline and a family tree, these could be group or class projects presented on charts and posted in the classroom for easy reference.

Students can note historic events on one side of the timeline and personal events on the other, using color coding and perhaps photographs.

# The Title of the Novel

*A Thousand Splendid Suns* takes its title from a poem describing Kabul by Saib-e-Tabriz, a 17th century Persian poet. The last two lines of this verse are quoted in two places in the novel:

> Every street of Kabul is enthralling to the eye
> Through the bazaars, caravans of Egypt pass
> One could not count the moons that shimmer on her roofs,
> Or the thousand splendid suns that hide behind her walls.

The poem recalls the past glories of Kabul - glories which the main characters (and the author) fervently hope will return.

The full text, translated by Josephine Davis, is available at http://webquestsplendidsuns. weebly.com/the-poem.html

*A Thousand Splendid Suns* by Khaled Hosseini

# Study Guide:

This novel deserves to be read *reflectively*. The questions are *not* designed to test you but to help you to locate and to understand characters, plot, settings, issues, and themes in the text. They do not normally have simple answers, nor is there always one answer. Consider a range of possible interpretations - preferably by *discussing* the questions with others. Disagreement is to be encouraged! Literary terms are underlined in the guide and definitions are provided at the end.

## PART ONE

The narrative is written in the third person but the focus is on Mariam: everything is seen from her perspective and she is the only character whose thoughts and feelings the narrator presents. All other characters are presented from the outside.

1. If you are familiar with Hosseini's first novel *The Kite Runner* then you know that he is deeply concerned with the gender inequalities in traditional Afghan society, and in particular with the double standards and hypocrisy concerning sexual conduct. The novel opens with a curse word, "harami" (bastard) shouted in frustration by Mariam's mother, when Mariam breaks the sugar bowl, one of Nana's few prized possessions. From the age of five, Mariam's sense of herself is defined and limited by her knowledge that she is illegitimate. The breaking of bowl that features a dragon on its side "meant to ward off evil" foreshadows Mariam's vulnerability - no one ever really protects her.

> 1. What precisely are the reasons for Nana's bitterness towards Jalil (who is, of course, the father of her "harami" (bastard) daughter Mariam)?
> 2. Mariam's mother tells her, "'Sometimes ... I wish my father had had the stomach to sharpen one of his knives and do the horrible thing'" (6). To what is she referring?

. As much as she loves her, for Nana, Mariam is a living symbol of her shame, a constant reminder that she is denied the status of a wife. Mariam is unable to verify the truth about her mother's version of the circumstances of her birth since her father Jalil gives her a very different, and much more positive, account.

15

3. Why does Mariam discount what Nana says in favor of Jalil's version? Who do you believe? Why?

**3.** Nana's reasons for rejecting Mariam's desire to attend school are many and various: some are purely selfish while others show a genuine concern for her daughter's wellbeing and happiness. Whatever their motivation, Nana's actions limit Mariam to being one of the oppressed for whom, in her mother's words, the only virtue worth learning is to "endure."

4. Make a list of reasons indicating what you take to be the motivation of each.

**4.** The fall of the monarchy places the lives of these individuals in their historical context: forces are about to impact them in ways they will be powerless to resist. This chapter is packed with rather ominous foreshadowing: Nana says that one day Mariam will "slip through his [Jalil's] fingers, hit the ground and break a bone. But Mariam did no believe that Jalil would drop her" (20). Mariam dreams that she and her father "would ride in his car, and people would point and say, 'There goes Jalil Khan with his daughter'" (23). The reader already understand enough about Jalil to realize that this will never happen.

5. Explain what it is that Mariam is failing to understand about her father?

**5.** Mariam tells Jalil and Nana that for her fifteenth birthday she wants to see a movie in her father's cinema and, moreover, that she wants to go with her other brothers and sisters. This naïve wish shows her total failure to understand her status as a bastard: her father may feel tenderly toward her, but he will never publically acknowledge her. Mariam shows great courage and determination in walking to Herat and staying all night outside her father's house, but she eventually has to accept that Nana was right about his determination to exclude her from his family. Her mother's suicide leaves Mariam alone, traumatized by her father's rejection of her and by the guilt she feels for abandoning Nana. Life has cruelly taught her that there is more truth to Nana's view of a bastard daughter's place in the world than there was in her father's stories.

6. What incident symbolizes the shattering of Mariam's hopes of being accepted as part of the family? [Clue: It happens as she is being carried to the car.]

7. How is Mariam treated by Jalil's servants? Explain how they treat her.

6. Following her mother's funeral, Mariam gets the very thing that she wished for when she is taken by Jalil to his house and given a room of her own. However, she now knows that she will never be accepted into the family, despite the kindness of her eight-year-old half-sister Nilofaur. Mariam holds herself responsible for her mother's suicide even though Mullah Faizullah tells her that her mother was unhappy even as a girl.

8. Comment on the statement "Jalil ... made a great show of tending to Mariam" (35).
9. Mariam is "startled awake by shouting" (39). Mariam cannot make out the words. What do you suppose is going on?
10. What is significant about the fact that Afsoon comes to Mariam's room for the first time to tell her that she is needed downstairs?

7. Jalil emerges as a very weak man who is completely dominated by his three wives: they want Mariam gone, and he acquiesces. Notice that Mariam is locked in her room: knowing that she is being forcibly married against her will, the wives make her literally a prisoner.

11. What elements of the arranged marriage system do Jalil's wives accept as normal (or at least pretend to accept as normal) that a Western reader would find totally unacceptable.
12. After her fate has been decided, there is this description, "Mariam looked down at the table ... every time she breathed out, the surface fogged, and she disappeared from her father's table." Analyze how this image communicates how Mariam is feeling about who she really is.

. It is very hard to see Jalil as a victim of Afghan values, but he is, for he as genuine feelings for Mariam that he is simply not brave enough to xpress because to do so would be to stand out against his culture. When Mariam tells him that she never wants him to visit her, he is devastated, though the reader probably feels little sympathy.

12. How does the narrative make it clear that it is the *abuse* of Islamic marriage that makes Mariam a victim?
13. Comment on this description, "Her own band [marriage ring] was a little tight, but Rasheed had no trouble forcing it over her knuckles" (49). What is foreshadowed here about Mariam's marriage?

**9. & 10.** Rasheed takes Mariam to Kabul where, for several days, she stays in her small room. After a week, he informs her that he expects her "'to start behaving like a wife'" (58). Mariam's upbringing has made her more strong-willed and independent than most women, yet she is unable to stand up against her husband and her growing understanding of his strict ideas of the role of a wife. To her surprise, Mariam takes pleasure when Rasheed compliments her cooking.

> 14. By Afghan standards, Rasheed is actually (at least for the first week) very patient and sensitive to Mariam's feelings. Give examples.

**11.** In the early 1970s, Kabul is a city where traditional and progressive notions of gender behaviors and relationships coexist. Rasheed is a traditionalist who is offended by the Westernized women in Kabul who go in public without covering their heads and even wear makeup. He insists that Mariam wears a burqa which she initially finds very strange. Later she actually finds it "comforting … Inside it, she was an observer buffered from the scrutinizing eyes of strangers" (66). Mariam has now cast off the identity of "bastard" for that of "wife." When Rasheed buys her a shawl she sees the gift as sincere. For the first time, Rasheed has sex with Mariam; it is not enjoyable for her, but she accepts it as part of her new role.

> 15. Again, Rasheed treats Mariam well, as though he is trying to form a relationship with her (albeit on his own terms as did Jalil). Give examples.
> 16. Mariam has been dreading her first experience of sex which proves to be loveless and painful: something that a man does to a woman. How much do you blame Rasheed for putting Mariam through this?
> 17. The chapter ends with a description of Mariam looking "at the frozen stars in the sky and a cloud that draped the face of the moon like a wedding veil." What does this imagery add to your understanding of how Mariam is feeling at this moment?

**12.** Rasheed begins to show signs of a more angry and violent side to his character which foreshadows misery for Mariam. There are a number of ominous signs (Rasheed's failure to participate in Ramadan, the picture of Rasheed and his wife, the pornography, and the gun), but Mariam ignores or excuses them all. Perhaps strangely, Mariam is described as feeling "Treasured and significant" as a result of Rasheed's "protectiveness" (74).

18. Explain why Mariam's sense of self-importance is elevated by the restrictions that Rasheed places on her.

19. List the things that Mariam finds in Rasheed's room and her reactions to each item. Comment on the last sentence of the chapter, "She told herself that they would make good companions after all" (77). How do you react to the way that she reacts?

13. At the start of this chapter, Mariam is at her most positive. In becoming pregnant, she has fulfilled her duty and her role. Rasheed is good to her. However, following the miscarriage, his attitude to her immediately changes because he blames her.

20. Water appears in a variety of forms in this chapter. Examine what, in each of its forms, it appears to <u>symbolize</u>.

21. How is Rasheed's hardening attitude to Mariam shown?

14. & 15. Mariam and Rasheed feel and express their grief at the loss of their baby in different ways. Mariam is eventually able to find comfort in religious faith, through prayer and the private burial of her unborn child. Rasheed, however, finds no outlet for his grief; he spends most of his time alone, refuses to have any part in the burial, and rebuffs Mariam when she reaches out to him by asking if she has angered him.

In April 1978 two things happen: Mir Akbar Khyber, a prominent communist is killed triggering a coup which overthrows President Daoud Khan and Fariba, a neighbor, gives birth to Laila the latest addition to her family. Rasheed hopes that the communist takeover will be good for a poor man like him, but the violence of the revolution is ominous. Fariba's fertility contrasts strongly with Mariam's seven miscarriages in four years of marriage.

22. Why does Mariam conduct a burial service for her prematurely aborted child? Why does Rasheed want nothing to do with it?

23. Rasheed forces Mariam to chew "a mouthful of grit and pebbles" because, he says, of her poor cooking (94). Where have pebbles been used before to symbolize the death of Mariam's dreams of a happy family life?

**PART TWO**

The narrative remains in the third person but the perspective changes from Mariam to Laila.

**16.** Laila's parents argue incessantly and have done so since her father, Hakim, allowed two of his sons, Ahmad and Noor, to join the fight against the Soviets. Fariba, Laila's mother, now regards her husband as weak and ineffectual.

> 24. How was the marriage of Laila's parents different when they were young? How and why has their relationship changed? How does their relationship affect Laila?
>
> 25. What is foreshadowed by the discussion of the three girls about "how to fend off unattractive suitors" (102)? Comment on Laila's confidence that her father is determined to ensure that she gets a good education.
>
> 26. What is the significance of the blue Mercedes Benz that Laila sees in the morning and the afternoon on her street?

**17.** Laila's mother fails to fetch her from school and without Tariq, her male friend, to protect her she is bullied. Fariba is still in bed: she clearly suffers from depression.

> 27. What is "'in *here*'"? Why does Fariba take no real interest in Laila?

**18.** Hakim is a progressive who gives credit to the communists for liberating women from the restrictions imposed on them by traditional Afghan culture. From him, Laila learns that Tariq's people, the Pashtuns, look down upon her people, the Tajiks, because historically Pashtuns have governed Afghanistan. When she is in Tariq's house, however, Laila feels neither tension nor resentment: she is always welcome.

> 28. Contrast the attitude toward the education of females which Laila and Mariam receive.
>
> 29. Why does Laila enjoy visiting Tariq's family? In what ways is Tariq's family different from her own?
>
> 30. What does Hakim mean when he tells Laila, "*the only enemy an Afghan cannot defeat is himself*" (122)?

**19. & 20.** News of the death of Ahmad and Noor sends Fariba deeper into depression. Though aware that she has failed Laila as a mother, Fariba cannot overcome her grief at the loss of her sons, a reflection of the unequal expectations of males and females in Laila's culture. Chapter five ends with a touching <u>simile</u> which encapsulates Laila's relationship with her mother.

**21.** Hakim takes Laila and Tariq on a trip to see the two giant Buddhas at Bamiyan which he tells Laila are part of Afghanistan's "heritage ... its rich past" (134). [You will need to do a little research on the fate of these two giant sculptures to answer the question that follows.]

31. Given their attitude to the two Buddhas, what is particularly ironic about the enthusiasm that the characters have for the Mujahideen in their battle against the Soviets and their high hopes following their victory?

32. During the afternoon Babi sits under an acacia tree re-reading Ernest Hemingway's novel
*The Old Man and the Sea*. If you are unfamiliar with this novel, look at the plot summary given on page 137. Why do you think that Laila's father is so drawn to this book.

**22. & 23.** Events move forward rapidly on both the personal and the political levels. Laila and Tariq are now adolescents (she is fourteen and he is sixteen). One of her friends is already married and another dreams of marrying soon. Fariba warns Laila about the need to avoid doing anything that will harm her reputation. Having lost Soviet support, President Najibullah surrenders putting an end to the communist regime and the Jihad. Afghanistan becomes the Islamic State of Afghanistan overseen by Jihad Council. Fariba recovers her spirits, but soon the Mujahideen, once united against the Soviets) falls into civil war.

33. In what ways does the fight between the men at the party foreshadow the future of Afghanistan and of the main characters in the story?

**24. & 25.** By June 1992, the fighting between the Wahdat and Pashtun factions is making Kabul a very dangerous place. Giti, Laila's childhood friend is blown apart on the street by a shell. Tariq tells Laila that he is leaving with his family. They have sex for the first time, but Laila knows she cannot accept his proposal of marriage because both her mother and father depend entirely on her. There is an obvious contrast between how Laila feels when she has sex for the first time and how Mariam felt.

34. Earlier, when Laila and Tariq "passed Rasheed, the shoemaker, and with his burqa-clad wife, Mariam, in tow … Rasheed had playfully said, 'If it isn't Laila and Majnoon,' referring to the star-crossed lovers of Nizami's popular twelfth-century romantic poem - a Farsi version of *Romeo and Juliet*" (148). Explain the significance that this remark now has.

26. Just as they are about to leave Laila's family home is struck by a shell She survives, but only just.

35. Explain the significance of the dream that Laila has (170-1).
36. How do you react to the description of the explosion?

# PART THREE

The <u>narrative voice</u> remains <u>third person limited</u>, but from this point on the perspective alternates between Mariam and Laila as indicated in the heading of each chapter.

**27. Mariam & 28. Laila**: Following the explosion which killed her father and mother, Rasheed found Laila under the rubble, dug her out with his bare hands, and brought her into the house. Mariam and Rasheed had taken care of Laila, nursed her wounds and given her pain-killing pills.

When she is somewhat recovered, Abdul Sharif, a stranger, comes to Rasheed's house. He tells her that he was in a bed in Peshawar hospital next to Tariq who had been injured by an attack on his refugee truck. Tariq asked Sharif to find Laila and tell her that he was thinking about her. Laila learns that Tariq died of his injuries.

37. How would you explain Rasheed's concern for the injured Laila?
38. Mariam asks Rasheed, "'How long is she staying?'" (180). What change does this suggest in Mariam's character?
39. Guilt has piled up in Laila's mind and at times she feels that the deaths of those closest to her are her fault. About what actions (and inactions) of her own does Laila feel guilty?

**29. Mariam & 30. Laila**: Rasheed (who is now sixty) tells lies to court Laila (much to the disgust of Mariam), but when she accepts his proposal she is also lying to him and will continue to do so.

40. Make a list of the deceptions that Laila perpetrates on Rasheed.
41. How would you describe Mariam's feelings about the marriage once it has taken place?

**1. Mariam**: Rasheed makes it clear to Laila that she is not to leave the house unless she is in his company and that even then case she must wear the burqa.

42. Why is Mariam so unsympathetic and unbending towards Laila?

**2. Laila & 33. Mariam**: As the civil war rages between the competing factions in the country and even in Kabul, so the animosity between Mariam and Laila continues despite the latter's attempts to reach an understanding with the older woman. They have a blazing row about a lost spoon. Laila gives birth to a girl whom she calls Aziza. This is a great disappointment to Rasheed who wanted a male heir. Relations between Rasheed and Laila deteriorate partly because Laila spends all of her time looking after the baby but mostly because she keeps refusing to have sex with him. Finally, Rasheed snaps and takes out his frustration on Mariam who he accuses of corrupting Laila. As he raised his belt to strike Mariam, Laila grabs his arm and holds on, thus saving the older woman. That night, Mariam finds Laila asleep and Aziza awake: she comforts the baby.

> 43. There are two incidents of one person holding onto another: Laila grabs Rasheed's arm and is swung off the ground; Aziza grabs Mariam's finger and Mariam does not try to pull it free. Comment on the importance and relationship of these two incidents.

**34. Laila & 35. Mariam**: Rasheed appears to grow suspicious about whether Aziza is his child because he questions Laila about her relationship with Tariq. Laila's act of protecting Mariam begins a thaw in their relations which blossoms into friendship even as the danger and violence in Kabul increases. Each tells the other the intimate details of their past and Laila reveals her plan to run away with Aziza in the spring. She asks Mariam to come with them.

> 44. Mariam experiences things that she has never experienced before and love and hope begin to grow in her. How does she explain the impact that Laila's protective action had on her? What does she get from Aziza that she has never had before?

**36. Laila**: Since the Mujahideen came to power in Kabul two years earlier strict Islamic Shari'a Law has been enforced. Women must wear the burqa and are forbidden to travel without a male relative. Lila and Mariam are betrayed by a man Laila asks to say he is her cousin and after being interrogated by the police the women are returned to Rasheed who take brutal revenge.

> 45. What is the first indication that the young man called Wakil is going to betray the two women?
> 46. At one point during her interrogation at the police station, "Laila almost laughed" (238). What is it that prompts this reaction?
> 47. How do you feel about the failure of Laila's escape plan? Did take you by surprise or did you see it coming? Explain.

**37. Mariam September 1996 & 38. Laila**: On September 27, 1996, the Taliban take over in Kabul having defeated the Mujahideen. Immediately they begin a reign of terror and repression: all men and women must adhere strictly to Shari'a Law or face brutal punishment. Rasheed warns Laila that all he has to do is report her to the authorities and she will be helpless. Laila knows herself to be pregnant with Rasheed's child and considers aborting the fetus but decides not to.

48. Of the rules propagated by the Taliban, which do you find the most shocking and why?
49. Explain clearly why Laila decides not to kill the baby growing in her womb.

**39. Mariam September 1997 & 40. Laila Fall 1999**: When Laila's time comes, Mariam and Rasheed take her to the old women's hospital but they are redirected to Rabia Balkhi hospital, the only one in Kabul staffed by women. The hospital is crowned and unequipped. When she finally sees a doctor Laila is told that she needs a cesarean operation immediately, but that there is no anesthetic.

Laila's son, Zalmai grows up to adore his father. Rasheed goes into debt to buy things for his son. His suggestion that Aziza be sent on the streets to beg results in a violent argument in which, for the first time, Laila strikes him and he threatens to shoot her.

50. As she struggles to get Laila treatment at the hospital, Mariam reflects that she understood "now the sacrifices a mother made" (256). Explain exactly what it is that she has understood and why.
51. The author rather cleverly keeps the reader in suspense about the purpose of the hole that Mariam and Laila are digging. How is this achieved?
52. What might Laila's dream of herself helplessly buying her own daughter foreshadow?

**1. Mariam**: It is 2000, a year of increasing drought and hardship in Kabul where, ironically, everyone is watching the film *Titanic* in secret since all movies are banned. The movie appears endlessly fascinating to the people of Kabul. When Rasheed's shop burns down the family quickly becomes destitute. Mariam makes an effort to contact her father, Jalil only to learn that he died in 1987.

53. *Titanic* is a symbol of Afghanistan. In what ways?
54. The appearance of the Mercedes Benz which Laila recognized outside Rasheed's house when she was a child is not explained. Why

had Jalil come to see Mariam? Why did she refuse to meet him and tear up the letter he wrote unread?

**42. Laila**: Rasheed's solution to lack of money is to have Aziza placed in an orphanage. Laila and Mariam are helpless to prevent this, but they are able to visit sometimes and Zaman, who runs the orphanage, is a kind man who believes in educating girls. Rasheed gets work as a doorman at the Intercontinental Hotel, and the family's financial problems ease a little. One day, Tariq (who Laila had been told was dead) turns up at their house.

55. What is the relationship between "what Aziza had said earlier about fractures and powerful collisions deep down" (290-1) and Aziza's stammer?

**43. Mariam & 44. Laila**: Mariam recalls that the doorman she had seen at the Intercontinental Hotel who looked vaguely familiar was the same man who called himself Abdul Sharif and told Laila of Tariq's terrible injuries and his death. Mariam realizes that Rasheed must have paid the man to lie to Laila.
Chapter 44 intersperses an account of Tariq's first visit with snippets of conversation from the evening. Tariq is able to tell Laila what had happened to him in the last decade, and Laila tells him about his daughter but, through Zalmai, Rasheed learns the identity of his wife's visitor.

56. The critic Raub interprets this chapter as an account of a series of visits paid by Tariq to Laila, "Throughout Tariq's and Laila's visits Zalmai tells Rasheed about 'mommy's new friend'. Rasheed figures out that Tariq is visiting Laila…" (GradeSaver). In the analysis offered above, I have interpreted it as the account of a single visit. Which interpretation do you favor and why?

**45. Mariam & 46. Laila**: To save Laila's life, Mariam kills Rasheed with the shovel. She explains to Laila what she has done and together they conceal the body in the toolshed. The following morning, Mariam tells Laila to take Zalmai and find Aziza and Tariq; she herself will stay and face justice for murdering Rasheed.

57. Why does Mariam sacrifice her life for Laila and the children? [Clue: There are many reasons - some to do with how Mariam has changed and some to do with the realities of the political situation.]

**47. Mariam**: The story of Mariam's trial, her period of imprisonment and her execution in the soccer stadium is told without romanticism or drama.

58. In her final moments, Mariam thinks, "This was a legitimate end to a life of illegitimate beginnings" (329). It is not immediately obvious what she means since the Taliban judicial system is anything but fair to women. Explain what you understand by Mariam's statement.

**PART FOUR**

The final part of the novel is written in the third person from the perspective of Laila.

**48. & 49.** Laila and Tariq Afghanistan take the two children to Murree, in Pakistani, where they are married. Tariq continues to word at Sayeed's hotel. In many ways life is good, but each of the four carries with them the traumas of their past. Following the 9/11 attacks, the Taliban rulers o Afghanistan refuse to turn over Osama bin Laden, claiming that it is against the Pashtunwali custom of hospitality, but Tariq is angry that the Taliban are distorting an honorable custom.

59. Explain the disagreement that Laila and Tariq have over the U.S invasion of Afghanistan.

**50.** After living for a year in Murree, Laila tells Tariq that she wants to return first to visit Herat and then to Kabul.

60. Explain Laila's longing to return to Kabul.

**51.** On the way to Kabul, Laila visits Herat, speaks with the son of Mulla Faizullah, and sees the *kolba* where Mariam spent the first fifteen years o her life. She also receives a locked box left by Jalil to be given to Mariam Hearing from her of Mariam's death, Mullah Faizullah's son gives it t Laila.

62. While visiting the *kolba* where Mariam lived, Laila has a vision c Mariam as a girl. Laila feels that "she sees something behind this girl' eyes … Something that, in the end, will be *her* undoing and Laila' salvation" (355). Explain exactly what quality it is that Laila perceive in Mariam and how it led to the outcome that it did.
63. Laila cannot understand the inclusion of the VCR of *Pinocchio* Explain why Jalil put it in the box.

**52. April 2003**: The drought in Kabul has broken, symbolizing th regeneration that is going on in the city. Laila, who teaches at th orphanage, and Tariq, who works with those disabled by the war fittin prosthetics, are part of this regeneration. Progress is fragile, however. O their way to the orphanage, Laila and her two children are nearly hit by a SUV driven by soldiers of one of the same war lords who caused so muc destruction in the past. Nevertheless, Laila is determined to rema hopeful, as is symbolized by the fact that she is pregnant.

64. The optimism of the novel's ending is heavily qualified. The story of Laila, Tariq, Aziza and Zalmai ends in April 2003. A great deal has happened in Afghanistan, and particularly in Kabul, since then. Do some research and then explain in detail what is likely to have happened to them, to the orphanage, and to the children (male and female) for whom they were caring.

65. Near the end of the chapter, we read, "Mariam is in Laila's own heart, where she shines with the bursting radiance of a thousand suns" (366). This is obviously an echo of the lines of the poem which give the novel its title:

> One could not count the moons that shimmer on her roofs,
> Or the thousand splendid suns that hide behind her walls.

How does the repetition of this metaphor bring together the themes of the novel?

**Glossary of literary terms (useful in discussing this novel)**

*first-person narrator/narrative* - The narrative in a work of fiction may either be third or first person. Third person narrative is told by an unidentified voice which belongs to someone not directly involved in the events narrated. First person narrative means that story is told from the necessarily limited viewpoint of one of the characters writing or speaking directly about themselves and their experience.

*foreshadowing* - An author uses foreshadowing when he/she hints at a future development in the plot. This builds up the reader's involvement in the fiction.

*image* - Imagery is a blanket term that describes the use of figurative language to represent objects, actions and ideas in such a way that i appeals to our five physical senses. Thus, amongst others, similes metaphors and symbolism are examples of images.

> *metaphor* - A metaphor is a implied comparison in which whateve is being described is referred to as though it were another thing (e.g., "To be, or not to be: that is the question: / Whether 'tis noble in the mind to suffer / The *slings and arrows* of outrageou *fortune*, / Or to take arms against *a sea of troubles*, / And b opposing end them?" Shakespeare *Hamlet*)

> *simile* - A simile is a descriptive comparison which uses the word "like" or "as" to make the intended comparison clear (e.g., "O m Luve's like a red, red rose / That's newly sprung in June; / O m Luve's like the melodie / That's sweetly play'd in tune." Robe Burns).

> *symbol* - A description in which one thing stand for or represen or suggests something bigger and more significant than itsel Normally a material object is used to represent an idea, belie action, theme, person, etc. (e.g., in the Burns poem above, he us the rose because it is a traditional symbol for love, passio emotion and romance just as the sun became a natural and almo universal symbol of kingship).

*irony / ironic* - The essential feature of irony is the presence of contradiction between an action or expression and the meaning it has the context in which it occurs. Writers are always conscious of usir irony, but there characters may either be aware or unaware that somethir that they say or do is ironic. Dramatic irony is the term used to describe character saying or doing something that has significance for the audien

A *Thousand Splendid Suns* by Khaled Hosseini

or reader but of which the characters are not aware. For example, when Othello says, "If it were now to die, / 'Twere now to be most happy, for I fear / My soul hath her content so absolute / That not another comfort like to this / Succeeds in unknown fate" (*Othello* 2:1), this is dramatic irony because the audience knows that he speaks truer than he knows.

*motivation* - Since Sigmund Freud 'invented' psychoanalysis, motivation has predominantly been though or in terms of psychology. Thus, the actions of a character may surprise us but they should also strike us as psychologically plausible.

A Study Guide

## Using the Study Guide Questions

Although there are both closed and open questions in the Study Guide, very few of them have simple, right or wrong answers. They are designed to encourage in-depth discussion, disagreement, and (eventually) consensus. Above all, they aim to encourage students to go to the text to support their conclusions and interpretations.

I am not so arrogant as to presume to tell teachers how they should use this resource. I used it in the following ways, each of which ensured that students were well prepared for class discussion and presentations.

**1.** Set a reading assignment for the class and tell everyone to be aware that the questions will be the focus of whole class discussion the next class.

**2.** Set a reading assignment for the class and allocate particular questions to sections of the class (e.g. if there are four questions, divide the class into four sections, etc.).

In class, form discussion groups containing one person who has prepared each question and allow time for feedback within the groups.

Have feedback to the whole class on each question by picking a group at random to present their answers and to follow up with class discussion.

**3.** Set a reading assignment for the class, but do not allocate questions.

In class, divide students into groups and allocate to each group one of the questions related to the reading assignment the answer to which they will have to present formally to the class.

Allow time for discussion and preparation.

**4.** Set a reading assignment for the class, but do not allocate questions.

In class, divide students into groups and allocate to each group one of the questions related to the reading assignment.

Allow time for discussion and preparation.

Now reconfigure the groups so that each group contains at least one person who has prepared each question and allow time for feedback within the groups.

**5.** Before starting to read the text, allocate specific questions to individuals or pairs. (It is best not to allocate all questions to allow for other approaches and variety. One in three questions or one in four seems about right.) Tell students that they will be leading the class discussion on the question. They will need to start with a brief presentation of the issues and then conduct a question and answer session. After this, they will be expected to present a brief review of the discussion.

5. Having finished the text, arrange the class into groups of 3, 4 or 5. Tell each group to select as many questions from the Study Guide as there are members of the group.

Each individual is responsible for drafting out a written answer to one question, and each answer should be a substantial paragraph.

Each group as a whole is then responsible for discussing, editing and suggesting improvements to each answer, which is revised by the original writer and brought back to the group for a final proof reading followed by revision.

This seems to work best when the group knows that at least some of the points for the activity will be based on the quality of all of the answers.

# Graphic organizer- Plot

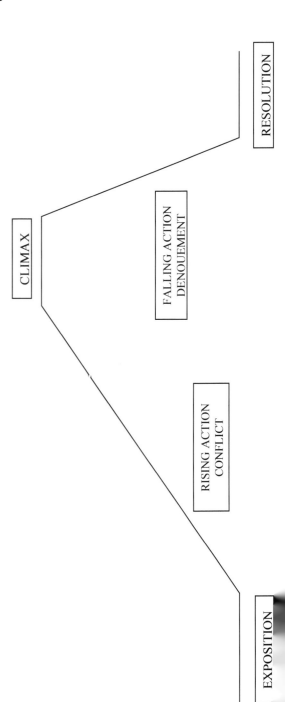

Plot graph for *A Thousand Splendid Suns*

*A Thousand Splendid Suns* by Khaled Hosseini

# Graphic organizer- Different perspectives

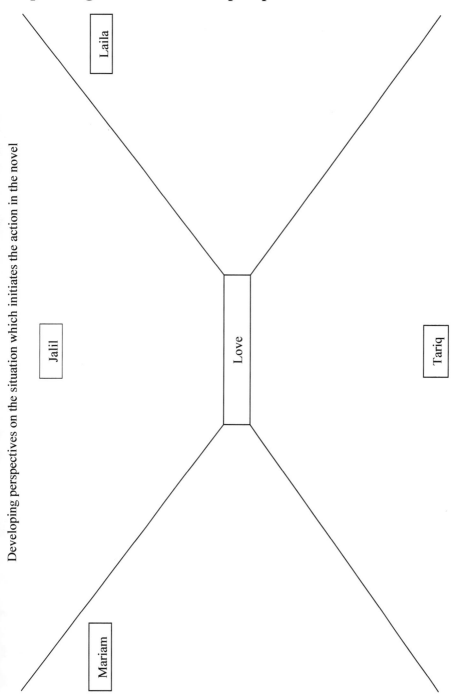

Developing perspectives on the situation which initiates the action in the novel

Laila

Jalil

Love

Tariq

Mariam

# Family Tree

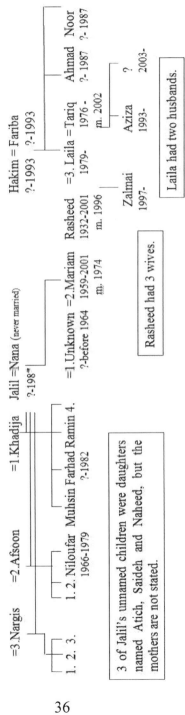

*A Thousand Splendid Suns family tree*

=3.Nargis     =2.Afsoon     =1.Khadija     Jalil =Nana (never married)
                               ?-198*

1. 2. 3.     1. 2. Niloufar Muhsin Farhad Ramin 4.
            1966-1979            ?-1982

3 of Jalil's unnamed children were daughters named Atich, Saideh and Naheed, but the mothers are not stated.

Hakim = Fariba
?-1993   ?-1993

=1.Unknown =2.Mariam    Rasheed     =3. Laila =Tariq    Ahmad   Noor
?-before 1964   1959-2001    1932-2001      1979-   1976-    ?-1987   ?-1987
           m. 1974       m. 1996              m. 2002

Rasheed had 3 wives.

Zalmai      Aziza      ?
1997-       1993-      2003-

Laila had two husbands.

# Timeline

| Afghanistan's history | Dates | | Events in the book |
|---|---|---|---|
| | | 1959 | Mariam is born. |
| Mohammed Daoud Khan declares himself President in a coup against the king, Mohammed Zahir Shah. | 17 July | 1973 | Ch. 1-4 detail Mariam's early life |
| | | 1974 | Ch. 5 Nana, Mariam's mother dies.<br>Ch. 8 Mariam marries Rasheed<br>Ch. 11 Rasheed makes Mariam wear the burqa.<br>Ch. 13 She becomes pregnant but miscarries. |
| | | 1976 | Ch. 23 Tariq is born |
| Saur Revolution: Military units loyal to the PDPA assaulted the Afghan Presidential Palace, killing President Mohammed Daoud Khan and his family. | 27 April | 1978 | Ch. 15 Mariam is now 19. She has miscarried 6 times.<br>Ch. 22 In October Laila is born. |
| Saur Revolution: The PDPA installed its leader, Nur Muhammad Taraki, as President of Afghanistan. | 1 May | | |
| A rebellion against the new Afghan government began with an uprising in Nuristan province. | July | | |

| | | | |
|---|---|---|---|
| A treaty was signed which permitted deployment of the Soviet military at the Afghan government's request. | 5 December | | |
| Taraki was murdered by supporters of Prime Minister Hafizullah Amin. | 14 September | 1979 | |
| *Soviet intervention* | | | |
| Soviet war in Afghanistan: Fearing the collapse of the Amin regime, the Soviet army invaded Afghanistan. | 24 December | | |
| Operation Storm-333: Soviet troops occupied major governmental, military and media buildings in Kabul, including the Tajbeg Palace, and executed Prime Minister Amin. | 27 December | | |
| | | 1981 | Ahmad and Noor, Laila brothers go off to fight th Soviets.<br>Tariq, aged 5, loses his le when he steps on landmine. (Ch. 18) |
| | | 1987 | Ch. 16 Laila is nine.<br>Ch. 18 She goes to scho and is bullied by Khadi until Tariq fights him.<br>Ch. 19 Laila's brothers a killed in the war |

| | | | Ch. 21 Laila, her father and Tariq visit the two Buddhas in Bamiyan Valley<br>Ch. 41 Jalil dies. |
|---|---|---|---|
| *Soviet war in Afghanistan*: The Soviet government signed the Geneva Accords, which included a timetable for withdrawing their armed forces. | 14 April | 1988 | |
| *Soviet war in Afghanistan*: The last Soviet troops left the country. | 15 February | 1989 | Ch. 22 January Tariq and Laila go to the cinema. Soviet troops are leaving Kabul. |

### Civil war

| | | | |
|---|---|---|---|
| *Civil war in Afghanistan (1989-1992)*: Afghan political parties signed the Peshawar Accord which created the Islamic State of Afghanistan and proclaimed Sibghatullah Mojaddedi as interim President. | 24 April | 1992 | Ch. 23 Tariq's father has had a series of strokes.<br>Ch. 24 Rocket attacks on Kabul.<br>Warlords rule areas of the city. Tariq gets a gun.<br>June - Pashtuns are fighting Hazaras.<br>Laila drops out of school and Babi teaches her at home.<br>Gita, Laila's friend is killed by a stray rocket<br>Ch. 25 -August Tariq and Laila make love. He asks her to marry him, but she refuses. |
| Gulbuddin Hekmatyar's Hezbi Islami, with the support of neighboring Pakistan, began a massive bombardment against the Islamic State in the capital Kabul. | | | Ch. 26 Tariq and his family leave for Pakistan. Laila |

39

| | | | |
|---|---|---|---|
| As agreed upon in the Peshawar Accord, Jamiat-e Islami leader Burhanuddin Rabbani took over as President. | 28 June | | and her family plan to leave Kabul, but their house is destroyed by a rocket. Ch. 27 Mariam and Rasheed care for Laila Ch. 28 Laila hears that Tariq is dead. Ch. 29 Rasheed plans to marry Laila (age 14) Ch. 30 Laila is pregnant so agrees to marry Rasheed. Mariam (age 33) and Laila come to an agreement. Ch. 32 Laila recalls her mother's friend Wajm talking about how Rasheed's son by his first wife drowned. |
| The Durand line Treaty is expired and all Afghans lands are supposed to be returned but Pakistan refuses to. | January | 1993 | Ch. 33 Aziza, a girl, is born. Laila saves Mariam from a beating. Ch. 34 Laila and Mariam reach an accord. |
| The Taliban government began to form in a small village between Lashkar Gah and Kandahar. | August | 1994 | Ch. 36 Laila tries to leave with Aziza and Mariam but they are betrayed Rasheed beats Mariam and locks Laila and Aziza in room without food or water. Ch. 37 Shari'a law detailed. |
| The Taliban, with Pakistani support, initiated a military campaign against the Islamic State of | January | 1995 | |

| | | | |
|---|---|---|---|
| Afghanistan and its capital Kabul. | | | |
| Taliban, tortured and killed Abdul Ali Mazari leader of the Hazara people. | 13 March | | |
| Civil war in Afghanistan (1996-2001): The forces of the Islamic State retreated to northern Afghanistan. | 26 September | 1996 | Ch. 38 Laila is pregnant by Rasheed. She thinks about aborting the baby. |
| The Taliban conquered Kabul and declared the establishment of the Islamic Emirate of Afghanistan. Former President Mohammad Najibullah, who had been living under United Nations protection in Kabul, was tortured, castrated and executed by Taliban forces. | 27 September | | |
| | | 1997 | Ch. 39 Laila has to get to a women's hospital to have her baby. The child, Zalmai, is born by Caesarean section with no anesthetic. |
| The Taliban captured Mazar-e Sharif, forcing Abdul Rashid Dostum to exile. | August | 1998 | |
| Cruise missile strikes in Afghanistan and Sudan (August 1998): | 20 August | | |

| | | | |
|---|---|---|---|
| Cruise missiles were fired by the United States Navy into four militant training camps in the Islamic Emirate of Afghanistan. | | | |
| | | 1999 | Ch. 40 Rasheed gets a black market TV. Mariam and Laila hide it in the garden because of Taliban searches. |
| | | 2000 | Ch. 41 Drought conditions Everyone is watching illici copies of Titanic. Rasheed's shop burn down. Mariam tries to get ai from her father, but he ha died.(1987) |
| Resistance leader Ahmad Shah Massoud was killed in a suicide bomb attack by two Arabs who disguised as French news reporters. | 9 September | 2001 | Ch. 42 Aziza placed in a orphanage because the have no income. Lai visits her daughter, but beaten if caught by th Taliban patrols. |
| After the September 11 attacks in the United States, U.S. President George W. Bush demanded the Taliban government to hand over al-Qaeda head Osama bin Laden and close all terrorist training camps in the country. | 20 September | | Rasheed gets a job as doorman. Tariq returns. Ch. 43 Mariam realize Rasheed arranged for Lai to hear Tariq was dead. Ch. 44 Tariq talks about h life Ch. 45 Zalmai reveals Lai met a man. Rasheed attacl her but he is killed l Mariam. |
| The Taliban refused Bush's ultimatum for | 21 September | | Ch. 46 Laila, Aziza ar |

*A Thousand Splendid Suns* by Khaled Hosseini

| | | | |
|---|---|---|---|
| ack of evidence connecting bin Laden o 9/11 attacks. | | | Zalmai leave. Ch. 47 Mariam is tried and executed at Ghazi Stadium Ch. 48 Tariq and Laila marry and live in Muree. Ch. 49 Afghanistan history |
| **US-led invasion** | | | |
| )peration Enduring 'reedom: The United States and the United Kingdom began an erial bombing ampaign against al-)aeda and the Taliban. | 7 October | | |
| he United Nations ecurity Council uthorized the creation f the International ecurity Assistance orce (ISAF) to help naintain security in fghanistan and assist ne Karzai dministration | 5 December | | |
| nternational onference on fghanistan in ermany: Hamid arzai chosen as head f the Afghan Interim dministration. | 20 December | | |
| oya jirga (grand sembly in Kabul): amid Karzai ppointed as President the Afghan ransitional | July | 2002 | Ch. 50 Lila and Tariq return to Herat and Kabul. In Herat Laila receives a box meant for Mariam from Mullah Faizullah's son. |

43

| | | | |
|---|---|---|---|
| Administration in Kabul, Afghanistan. | | | |
| A 502-delegate loya jirga was held to consider a new Afghan constitution. | 14 December | 2003 | Ch. 51 Laila is teaching a the orphanage Tariq works with the disabled Laila is pregnant with he third child. |
| **Elections** | | | |
| Hamid Karzai was elected President of the Islamic Republic of Afghanistan after winning the Afghan presidential election. | 9 October | 2004 | |

The section of the timeline that deals with Afghan history is very slightl adapted from the Wikipedia article "Timeline of Afghan history." (It i reproduced on the basis of the Creative Commons License http://creativecommons.org/licenses/by-sa/3.0/)

# Further Reading

**Hosseini's first novel, *The Kite Runner* (2003),** is the story of two half-brothers who grow up together as playmates in Afghanistan and whose lives become entwined in tragic ways. Baba (no other name is given) is a highly successful businessman in Kabul: Amir is his legitimate son whose mother died in childbirth; Hassan is his illegitimate son conceived during an affair between Baba and the wife of his servant Ali, a fact which has been kept a closely guarded secret. Shortly after his birth, Hassan's mother ran out on the family, so both boys grow up without the love of a mother. Amir is an excellent competitive kite flyer and Hassan is the greatest kite runner in Kabul. (Kite runners attempt to capture the downed kites as victory trophies.) After one important kite battle that Amir wins, he witnesses his friend Hassan being attacked by three of the neighborhood boys, one of whom rapes him. Amir stands by and does nothing because he is too scared to intervene. He then has his former friend sent away by Baba on a false charge of theft, but he will feel the guilt of his cowardice and his lie for the rest of his life.

Baba and Amir emigrate from Afghanistan to California where Amir gets married and begins to make a career as a novelist. When he returns to Afghanistan, he finds that Hassan is dead but that his son, Sohrab, needs protection. Perhaps now he will be able to atone for his failure to save Hassan.

## Works Cited

You should certainly read the two interviews listed below.]

An Interview with Khaled Hosseini." *Book Browse*, 2007. Web. July 24, 2015.

Oley, Dylan. "Interview / Khaled Hosseini: Two Afghan wives salvage joy amid strife." *The Denver Post Search*, July 15, 2007. Web. July 24, 2015.

Hosseini, Khaled. *A Thousand Splendid Suns*. 1st Edition. New York: Riverhead Books, 2007. Print.

Raub, Adena and Chainani, Soman ed. "A Thousand Splendid Suns." GradeSaver, 13 June 2008 Web. 19 July 2015.

**Arabic/ Persian Glossary**

Afghanistan is a multilingual country.
Pashto and Dari are the most widely spoken.

*Agha:* honorific title for a civilian also a title used by Pashtun warlords
*Aftawa:* bowl
*Ahmaq*: a fool
*Aishee*: milk
*Akhund*: Muslim teacher
*Alef, beh, seh: a, b, c*
*Allah u akbar:*
*Alhamdulellah*: "All praise and thanks to God"
*Almari*: chest of drawers
*Ambagh*: shares the same husband
*Ameer-ul-Mumineen*: Leader of the Faithful (a.k.a Mullah Omar)
*Aneh*: strange
*Arbab*: village leader
*Aroos:* daughter-in-law
*Aush*: Afghan soup dish made with noodles and different vegetables in a tomato-based broth
*Aushak:* pasta dumplings filled with scallion, with a minced beef sauce
*Azan*: call to prayer

\*\*\*

*Babaloo:* type of prayer
*Bacha*: boy
*Badmash*: naughty or bad
*Balay:* yes
*Bas*: enough

*Bebakhsh:* I'm sorry?
*Beid*: type of tree
*Bia*: come
*Bismallah-e-rahman-e-rahims*: in honour of our beloved prophet
*Biwa:* widow
*Borani*: Iranian appetizer
*Bov*: bus
*Burqa*: head-to-toe covering worn by women
*Buzkashi*: national sport of Afghanistan, played on horseback, involve capturing a goat or cal carcass and dropping into a scoring circle.

\*\*\*

*Chai*: tea
*Chaman*: the capital of Qil Abdullah distric Baluchistan, Pakistan
*Chapan*: coat adorned wit intricate threading wo over clothes, usual during the cold wint months and usually t men
*Chapli kebab:* a minced be patty served with naa bread. Chapli means fl and derives from t Pashto word

46

*Chaprikh*: common dish in Pashtun cuisine.

*Chelo kebab:* the national dish of Iran. It is served on skewers on a bed of rice.

*Chup ko*: shut up

\*\*\*

*Daal*: a stew

*Degeh*: else

*Dehati*: village girl

*Didi*: an affectionate word used by mothers

*Dil*: the heart, courage.

*Dishlemeh:* cup of tea with a sugar cube in the saucer

*Diwana*: crazy

*Dogh*: yogurt drink

*Dohol:* large cylindrical drum with two skin heads, one at each end

*Dokhtar e jawan*: young woman

*Dokhtar jan* or *dokhtar jo* (different dialect)– daughter, girl

*Dootar:* long-necked two-stringed lute

*Dozd*: thief

\*\*\*

*Eid mubarak*: traditional Muslim greeting reserved for the use on the festivals of Eid ul-Adha and Eid ul-Fitr.

*Eid- ul Fitr*: The celebration that marks the end of the month of Ramadan, Eid is marked by the sighting of the new moon. Eid lasts three days and is celebrated with festivities and merriment. Special prayers and rituals are associated with the three day observance.

*Espand:* herb for burning

\*\*\*

*Fahmidi:* "You don't understand."

*Fatiha*: a funeral

\*\*\*

*Gap bezan*: "Say something."

*Garis*: carriage/ horse-drawn cart

*Ghazals*: poetry

*Goh*: feces

*Gul*: flower

\*\*\*

*Halwa*: dense, sweet confection

*Hamam*: public bathhouse

*Hamshira* or *hamshireh* (different dialect): sister

*Hamwatan*: person

*Harami:* bastard child.

*Hashish*: narcotic drug made from compressed cannabis

*Hazaras*: People who inhabit the central region of Afghanistan and speak Persian, most of whom are Shia Muslims.

47

*Hijab*: veil that covers the head and chest, which is often worn by Muslim women beyond the age of puberty in the presence of adult males

\*\*\*

*Iftar*: meal that breaks the fast of Ramadan;
*Ikhlas*: 112th Sura of the Koran
*Inqilabi*: revolutionary
*Inshallah*: God willing
*Ishtop:* heater

\*\*\*

*Jan* or *Jo* (different dialect): dear
*Jelabi*: doughnut
*Jihad*: Holy War
*Jinn*: supernatural demon in Islamic mythology

\*\*\*

*Kafir*: infidel
*Kaka*: uncle
*Kenarab*: a shit hole
*Khala*: aunt
*Khar:* donkey
*Khastegar:* marriage suitor
*Khatm:* final
*Khayat*: tailor, seamstress
*Khila:* half-wit, stupid
*Khodaya:* "Oh God!"
*Khosh Shodi:* happy now
*Kichiri:* rice and lentils
*Kinchini:* spoiled
*Kolba*: shack or hut.
*Koran* or *Qu'ran*: the Islamic holy book

\*\*\*

*La Illah u ilillah:* "There is no God but God"
*Lagaan*: tub
*Lotfan*: please
*Loya Jirga*: Grand Assembly

\*\*\*

*Mahram*: male relative
*Malika*: queen
*Mantu:* a food
*Mashallah*: expression of respect appreciation o thankfulness
*Mastawa*: Afghan mea comprised of rice with lamb and chickpeas
*Moalim:* teacher
*Moochi*: beggar, ordinary perso
*Mozaham*: bother
*Mujahideen*: guerrilla typ military outfits led b Muslim afghan warrio in the soviet war i Afghanistan, but late fought each other.
*Mullah:* title of respect for person learned in sacre law

\*\*\*

*Na fahmidi*: "Did yc understand?"
*Namaz:* prayer
*Namoos*: pride
*Nang*: honor
*Nau Socha*: good as new
*Nay*: no

*Nikka*: marriage ceremony
*Noor:* light

\*\*\*

*Pahlawan*: great warrior
*Pakol*: soft, rounded, afghan or Pashtun man's hat, usually wool and an earthy color
*Pakora:* fried snack
*Panjpar*: card game
*Pari :* beauty
*Pashtun*wali: code of conduct
*Poostin* or *Poosteen*: type of coat

\*\*\*

*Qanoon*: law
*Qurma*: stew

\*\*\*

*Rafiq:* friend
*Ramadan*: one-month Islamic spiritual observance involves fasting (between sunrise and sundown).
*risha*: (family) roots
*rubab*: musical instrument
*ruqats:* parts

\*\*\*

*sabzi*: stew
*salaam*: salutation
*saratan:* June/ July
*sawab*: good deed, reward
*shaheed*: martyr
*shahnai*: type of oboe, made from wood
*shalqam*: stew

*Sharab:* alcohol
*Shari'a:* the Islamic legal system derived from the religious precepts of Islam
*Shorwa*: a simple soup eaten in Afghanistan
*Sofrah*: a spread of edible items laid out on a cloth on the floor or on a low table
*Sujda:* a prayer stance
*Surrah*: parts of the Koran

\*\*\*

*Tabreek:* congratulations.
*Tahamul:* endure
*Tambouras:* musical instrument
*Tajik*: a minority group of Afghanis who speak the Persian language
*Taliban:* Sunni extremist group which controlled Afghanistan from 1996-2001
*Tasbeh*: repetitive utterances as moving beads on a necklace
*Tashakor:* "Thank you."
*Tumban:* traditional attire

\*\*\*

*Wah:* "Bravo!"
*Wahshis:* savages
*Wallah:* a person who performs a specific task
*Wallah o billah:* "Never a moment's rest"

\*\*\*

*Yaklenga*:  cripple

*** 

*Zahmat:*  trouble, work

***


(This glossary has been composed from a number of sources.)

*A Thousand Splendid Suns* by Khaled Hosseini

# To the Reader

Ray strives to make his products the best that they can be. If you have any comments or questions about this book *please* contact the author through his email: **moore.ray1@yahoo.com**

Visit his website at **http://www.raymooreauthor.com**

**Also by Ray Moore:** Most books are available from amazon.com as paperbacks and at most online eBook retailers.

## Fiction:

***The Lyle Thorne Mysteries:*** each book features five tales from the Golden Age of Detection:

*Investigations of The Reverend Lyle Thorne*
*Further Investigations of The Reverend Lyle Thorne*
*Early Investigations of Lyle Thorne*
*Sanditon Investigations of The Reverend Lyle Thorne*
*Final Investigations of The Reverend Lyle Thorne*

## Non-fiction:

The ***Critical Introduction series*** is written for high school teachers and students and for college undergraduates. Each volume gives an in-depth analysis of a key text:

*"The Stranger" by Albert Camus: A Critical Introduction* (Revised Second Edition)
*"The General Prologue" by Geoffrey Chaucer: A Critical Introduction*
*"Pride and Prejudice" by Jane Austen: A Critical Introduction*
*"The Great Gatsby" by F. Scott Fitzgerald: A Critical Introduction*

The ***Text and Critical Introduction series*** <u>differs</u> from the Critical introduction series as these books contain the original text and in the case of the medieval texts an interlinear translation to aid the understanding of the text. The commentary allows the reader to develop a deeper understanding of the text and themes within the text.

*"Sir Gawain and the Green Knight": Text and Critical Introduction*
*"The General Prologue" by Geoffrey Chaucer: Text and Critical Introduction*
*"The Wife of Bath's Prologue and Tale" by Geoffrey Chaucer: Text and Critical Introduction*
*"Heart of Darkness" by Joseph Conrad: Text and Critical Introduction*
*"The Sign of Four" by Sir Arthur Conan Doyle Text and Critical Introduction*
*"A Room with a View" By E.M. Forster: Text and Critical Introduction*

**Study guides available in print- listed alphabetically by author**

51

# A Study Guide

*denotes also available as an eBook*

"Wuthering Heights" by Emily Brontë: A Study Guide *

"Jane Eyre" by Charlotte Brontë: A Study Guide *

"The Meursault Investigation" by Kamel Daoud: A Study Guide

"Great Expectations" by Charles Dickens: A Study Guide *

"The Myth of Sisyphus" and "The Stranger" by Albert Camus: Two Study Guides *

"The Sign of Four" by Sir Arthur Conan Doyle: A Study Guide *

"A Room with a View" by E. M. Forster: A Study Guide

"Looking for Alaska" by John Green: A Study Guide

"Paper Towns" by John Green: A Study Guide

"Unbroken" by Laura Hillenbrand: A Study Guide

"The Kite Runner" by Khaled Hosseini: A Study Guide

"On the Road" by Jack Keruoac: A Study Guide

"The Secret Life of Bees" by Sue Monk Kidd: A Study Guide

"An Inspector Calls" by J.B. Priestley: A Study Guide

"Macbeth" by William Shakespeare: A Study Guide *

"Othello" by William Shakespeare: A Study Guide *

"Antigone" by Sophocles: A Study Guide *

"Oedipus Rex" by Sophocles: A Study Guide

"Cannery Row" by John Steinbeck: A Study Guide

"Of Mice and Men" by John Steinbeck: A Study Guide *

## Study Guides available as e-books:

"Heart of Darkness" by Joseph Conrad: A Study Guide

"The Mill on the Floss" by George Eliot: A Study Guide

"Lord of the Flies" by William Golding: A Study Guide

"Catch-22" by Joseph Heller: A Study Guide

"Life of Pi" by Yann Martel: A Study Guide

"Nineteen Eighty-Four by George Orwell: A Study Guide

"Selected Poems" by Sylvia Plath: A Study Guide

"Henry IV Part 2" by William Shakespeare: A Study Guide

"Julius Caesar" by William Shakespeare: A Study Guide

"The Pearl" by John Steinbeck: A Study Guide

"Slaughterhouse-Five" by Kurt Vonnegut: A Study Guide

"The Bridge of San Luis Rey" by Thornton Wilder: A Study Guide

**Teacher resources:** Ray also publishes many more study guides and other resources for classroom use on the 'Teachers Pay Teachers' website: **http://www.teacherspayteachers.com/Store/Raymond-Moore**

Made in the USA
Middletown, DE
20 September 2019